Arrête pas la musique!

PORTRAITS OF SOUTH LOUISIANA

Front cover: Morris and Alphonse Ardoin, Mamou, Louisiana, 1998

Back cover: Ambrose Thibodeaux, Lafayette, Louisiana, 1982

© 2017 by University of Louisiana at Lafayette Press
All rights reserved
ISBN 13 (paper): 978-1-946160-05-8

http://ulpress.org
University of Louisiana at Lafayette Press
P.O. Box 43558
Lafayette, LA 70504-3558

Printed on acid-free paper in Canada

Library of Congress Cataloging-in-Publication Data

Names: Waagenaar, Emile, 1949- author.
Title: Arrête pas la musique! : portraits of South Louisiana / Emile Waagenaar.
Description: Lafayette, LA : University of Louisiana at Lafayette Press, 2017.
Identifiers: LCCN 2017025955 | ISBN 9781946160058
Subjects: LCSH: Musicians--Louisiana--Portraits.
Classification: LCC ML87 .W33 2017 | DDC 781.62/410763--dc23
LC record available at https://lccn.loc.gov/2017025955

Arrête pas la musique!

PORTRAITS OF SOUTH LOUISIANA

PHOTOGRAPHY BY EMILE WAAGENAAR | FOREWORD BY ANN SAVOY

University of Louisiana at Lafayette Press
2017

Ann Savoy. Photo by Gabrielle Savoy, Eunice, Louisiana, 2014

Ann Savoy is a musician, an author, a record producer, and a photographer. She plays guitar, fiddle, and accordion, and has traveled throughout the world with the Savoy-Doucet Cajun Band, the Savoy Family Band, and her Grammy-nominated band The Magnolia Sisters. She is the author of the Botkin Award-winning book, *Cajun Music: A Reflection of a People*, and she has also written book chapters, liner notes, and articles on Cajun music

FOREWORD

Emile Waagnaar came to a jam session at our music store, Savoy Music Center, in Eunice, Louisiana, one day in 1997. As he enjoyed the music and atmosphere of the 1960s accordion shop, he quietly told me that he was a photographer and had some photos to show me. Over the past forty years many photographers have come through our doors, many great photographers, many just curious documenters. Emile had a friendly look on his face, but also a look of studying a situation, as if he was looking at the world through a camera frame. Though I didn't yet know it, something told me that this was not your average photographer.

My instincts were correct. When Emile let me look through his photos they weren't just pictures of people. They were studies of the people. Somehow he managed to place the musicians he was photographing in a setting that told a little about who they are. For example, accordionist/accordion builder Don Montoucet is seen in his accordion workshop surrounded by taxidermy animal heads. The ever energetic Joel Sonnier is posed on an exercise bike playing his accordion. Stark landscapes are sharply documented just as stark as they are, revealing the hard flat light of midday south Louisiana. Through Emile's eye, the quirky world of southwest Louisiana unfolds in all its inexplicable joy and weirdness.

Emile hails from the Netherlands, so perhaps I can go so far as to say he is creating photographic Dutch interiors, letting the setting show a little of the subjects' inner world. Some of the photos made me laugh because they showed little surprising things about the subjects. Many were tender. There was also romance. A wide gamut of types of Louisiana places and people are documented here, not just pretty things and people, but also well worn and hard worked subjects.

Emile's photos are a unique take on a frequently photographed world, an intimate look inside the lives of the subjects, a journey into places that not many photographers are allowed to go, or even think to go. The photograph is a rendering of a split second for all eternity, and in these photographic seconds Emile has shown us what he sees here; the result being an intimate and sometimes strange trip through wonderful French Louisiana.

–Ann Savoy, Eunice, Louisiana, 2017

Emile Waagenaar in street mirror, Lafayette, France, 2015

INTRODUCTION

I first stood on Louisiana soil in Lafayette during May of 1982. There, I found myself standing at the crossroads of another culture. Shortly after, I heard about a Clifton Chenier gig scheduled for the next day at the Grant Street Dancehall. Clifton was very ill and could not perform that night, so Rockin' Dopsie filled in. That evening someone gave me Ambrose Thibodeaux's name and address written on a paper napkin. This is how it went every trip I took—acquiring names of musicians scribbled on little pieces of paper or cardboard beer coasters.

On a Sunday afternoon during that same trip, I met Riley and Ruby Domingue at Alex Broussard's Dance Hall in Scott. I wasn't paying attention to where I was going while photographing, and I accidentally tipped over the table where they were sitting. Beer spilled all over the dance floor, so I offered to buy them a new round, but they declined my offer and instead bought one for me! They invited me to their home in Rayne, and with Riley I was introduced to some giants of Cajun music, such as Aldus Roger and Leroy "Happy" Fats Leblanc. The Domingue family provided a significant source of information for locating musicians during my first trips to Louisiana.

This is my story—how I discovered Cajun music and its musicians. Several times I went back; time and again I was surprised by the cultural endurance of this relatively small group of people. Both old and young keep their history alive through a simple bond—the culture, the language, and the songs of their ancestors. But I also discovered some places in France, such as "La Ligne Acadienne," where the ancestors of the Cajuns lived centuries ago, before they decided to build a new life in another world. This is not a historical document about these people and their music, and it is far from complete when it comes to even musicians. These images instead record my journey into a culture that continually captivates me.

–Emile Waagenaar, Breda, the Netherlands, March 2017

FROM FRANCE TO LOUISIANA

The Cajuns trace their history back to French people who left their homes in the 1600s and ventured to Acadie (today's Nova Scotia, Canada). Among these migrants were carpenters, notaries, and even prostitutes. Later, many French farmers and fishermen also went to Acadie. They originated mainly from Normandy, Brittany, Vendée, and Poitou-Charentes, and their descendants would become known as the Acadians.

In 1755, the British, who had taken control of Acadie earlier in the eighteenth century, began dispersing Acadians across North America and Europe. In 1774, one group of refugees ended up back in France. The Marquis de Pérusse d'Escars built them 150 farms near Archigny, in an area still known as "La Ligne Acadienne." Each family got a house, a harrow, a plow, a wagon, two oxen, two cows, and forty-two acres of land. Some of the buildings are still standing, although the houses are more often used as barns today.

For some members of this group of Acadians in France, as well as for others scattered around the northern Atlantic, Spanish Louisiana beckoned as an attractive option for resettlement. Originally founded as a French colony, its inhabitants shared a language and religion with the dispersed Acadians. They began arriving in Louisiana as early as the mid-1760s, with more groups coming sporadically through the 1780s. The colonial government settled them along the bayous and prairies of south Louisiana, where over time they developed a distinctive culture and became known as Cajuns. Influenced by neighboring black Creoles among others, and bringing their own historical references to the table, by the twentieth century these Cajuns created music rooted in its heritage yet almost constantly evolving. They still stretch the boundaries of so-called traditional music to this day.

Saint Jehan passenger registration list from 1636 with the names of several early settlers to Acadie, Archives Départementales de Charente Maritime, La Rochelle, France, 2015

La Rue "sur les murs," La Rochelle, Charente-Maritime, France, 2015

Grand Rue, Beauvoir sur Mer, Vendée, France, 2015

4

Fishing nets near Beauvoir sur Mer, Vendée, France, 2015

Saltfields near Beauvoir sur Mer, Vendée, France, 2015

La Ligne Acadienne, Archigny, Vienne, France, 2015

Maison Acadienne 1774, Farm 17, Archigny, Vienne, France, 2015

Farmhouse, now sheep barn and hay shed, on "La Ligne Acadienne" near Archigny, Vienne, France, 2015. Francois Daigle and Jeanne Holley lived here in 1774.

Bay Hebert with his two mules plowing his land in the neighborhood of Carencro, Louisiana, 1998

12

Grain fields with granary and rain showers near Archigny, Vienne, France, 2015

Rice mill near Kaplan, Louisiana, 2001

Holly Beach, Gulf Beach Highway, Cameron, Louisiana, 1982

A Cajun Hi-Rise house near Cameron, Louisiana, 2008. After Hurricane Rita, in September 2005, houses had to be rebuilt higher because of the insurance.

Beach House, near Cameron, Louisiana, 1982

Ferry *Cameron*, Holly Beach, Louisiana, 1982

LA 82 passes the Rockefeller State Wildlife Refuge, near Grand Chenier, Louisiana, 1982

Crossroad of Evangeline Drive and Cameron Street, Lafayette, Louisiana, 1982

Riley and Ruby Domingue with grandson Cody in Rayne, Louisiana, 1989

Grant Street Dance Hall, Lafayette, Louisiana, 1982

Grant Street Dance Hall with Rockin' Dopsie & Zachary Richard, Lafayette, Louisiana, 1982

Ambrose Thibodeaux, Lafayette, Louisiana, 1982

Matthew Courville in front of the Liberty Theater in Eunice, Louisiana, 1997

Fred's Lounge, Mamou, Louisiana, 1982

"Tante" Sue and Fred Tate, Fred's Lounge, Mamou, Louisiana, 1989

Fred Tate, Fred's Lounge, Mamou, Louisiana, 1982

"Tante" Sue, Fred's Lounge, Mamou, Louisiana, 2008

Fred's Lounge, Kurt Daigle and friends on a Saturday morning round 10:30 a.m., Mamou, Louisiana, 2006

MARDI
GENUINE DRAFT
GRAS
2005
Fred's

Fred's Lounge, Sady Courville and Roy Fusilier, Ambrose Thibodeaux dancing in the back, Mamou, Louisiana, 1982

Hotel Cazan, Mamou, Louisiana, 1998

Hotel Cazan, Mamou, Louisiana, 2006

Hotel Cazan, Mamou, Louisiana, 2008

Crawfish Festival, Breaux Bridge, Louisiana, 1982

Robert Dafford, selling posters and paintings in a caravan at Route 94 near Breaux Bridge, Louisiana, 1982

Crawfish Festival, Breaux Bridge, Louisiana, 1982

Visitors at Crawfish Festival, Breaux Bridge, Louisiana, 1982

Crawfish hat seller, Crawfish Festival, Breaux Bridge, Louisiana, 1982

Chris and Dolly at the Alex Broussard Dance Hall, Scott, Louisiana, 1982

38

Lee Lavergne, Lanor Records, Church Point, Louisiana, 1997

Leroy Broussard at the Alex Broussard Dance Hall, Scott, Louisiana, 1982

Christine Balfa dancing with Jean Ancelet, Festival Acadiens, Lafayette, Louisiana, 1998

Steve Riley & The Mamou Playboys, Festival Acadiens, Lafayette, Louisiana, 1939

42

D'Jalma Garnier, Carencro, Louisiana, 2008

Jesse Lége behind the Liberty Theater in Eunice, Louisiana, 2008

Paul Daigle, Pointe Noir, Louisiana, 2008

Orsy Vanicor, Welsh, Louisiana, 2008

Eddie LeJeune and Emerson Jr., Morse, Louisiana, 1998

Mee-Mee's Café, Morse, Louisiana, 2008

48

Hubert Maitre, Scott, Louisiana, 2001

Leo Abshire, Kaplan, Louisiana, 1998

50

Ervin LeJeune, Lake Charles, Louisiana, 2008, Ervin plays on his father's, Iry LeJeune, fiddle; on the table sits Iry's accordion

Eddie Shuler, Goldband Records, Lake Charles, Louisiana, 1982

Ellis Vanicor, Lacassine, Louisiana, 2008

Milton and Odile Vanicor, Welsh, Louisiana, 2008

Dirk Powell and Christine Balfa, St. Martinville, Louisiana, 1998

J.C. Melancon, Cecilia, Louisiana, 2008

Railroad Crossing, Nederland, Texas, 2008

Rodney LeJeune, Nederland, Texas, 2008

58

Larry G. Miller, Iota, Louisiana, 1982

Jay Miller, Bon Tee Accordions, Iota, Louisiana, 2008

60

Ken Smith, Kinder, Louisiana, 2008

Luderin Darbone, Sulphur, Louisiana, 1982

Cajun Flea Market, Lafayette, Louisiana, 1982

Boys in front of shop window at Cajun Flea Market, Lafayette, Louisiana, 1982

Morris and Dexter Ardoin, Eunice, Louisiana, 1998

Morris and Alphonse Ardoin, "Bois Sec," Mamou, Louisiana, 1998

Kerry Boutté, owner of Mulate's Restaurant, Breaux Bridge, Louisiana, 1989

Octa Clark with tourist at Mulate's Restaurant, Breaux Bridge, Louisiana, 1989

68

Philip Gould, photographer, Lafayette, Louisiana, 2001

Horace Trahan standing in front of a picture of his uncle Felix Richard, photographed by Philip Gould, Lafayette, Louisiana, 1998

Errol Verret and Tony Latiolais, St. Martinville, Louisiana, 1997

Greg Guirard, photographer, St. Martinville, Louisiana, 1997

72

Leroy "Happy Fats" LeBlanc, Rayne, Louisiana, 1982

Lee Benoit, Rayne, Louisiana, 2001

Brooke Henry, Miss Swine, with bullfrog at the Frog Festival in Rayne, Louisiana, 1997

Myrta Fair Bradbury Craig, Director of the Rayne *Acadian Tribune* and organizer of the Frog Festival, Rayne, Louisiana, 1982

Allen Richard, Gueydan, Louisiana, 2001

Wayne Toups, backstage at Frog Festival, Rayne, Louisiana, 1997

80

Roddie Romero, Lafayette, Louisiana, 1997

Ophe Romero, accordion, and his brother Lennis Romero, "t-fer," known as the Romero Brothers, St. Martinville, Louisiana, 2001

82

Ray Abshire, Lafayette, Louisiana, 2006

Cory and Lisa McCauley, Mamou, Louisiana, 1998

David Greely, Breaux Bridge, Louisiana, 2008

L.J. Hebert, Kaplan, Louisiana, 2001

86

Carol Rachou, La Louisianne Records, Lafayette, Louisiana, 1982

Adam Hebert and Cleveland Dupuis, Lafayette, Louisiana, 2008

Bobby Charles, Abbeville, Louisiana, 1989

Bobby Charles, Abbeville, Louisiana, 1989

90

Hector Duhon, Lafayette, Louisiana, 1989

Al Berard, Cecilia, Louisiana, 2008

Sheryl Cormier, Carencro, Louisiana, 1997

Doris Leon "D.L." Menard, Erath, Louisiana, 1997

Kevin Naquin and his two daughters, Lafayette, Louisiana, 2001

Don Montoucet, Scott, Louisiana, 2008

Merlin Fontenot, Lafayette, Louisiana, 1997

Leola Denson-Thibodeaux, Lafayette, Louisiana, 1997

Floyd Soileau, Swallow Records, Ville Platte, Louisiana, 1998

J.C. Soileau, Ville Platte, Louisiana, 1998

100

Rodney Fontenot, Eunice, Louisiana, 2008

Kira Viator, Crowley, Louisiana, 1998

Ann Savoy, Eunice, Louisiana, 2008

Marc Savoy, Acadian Accordions, Eunice, Louisiana, 2001

Philosophical expressions of Marc on the doors of his work cabinets, 2001

104

Kevin Wimmer, Breaux Bridge, Louisiana, 2008

Nonc Allie Young and his wife Viola, Basile, Louisiana, 2001

Steve Riley, Lafayette, Louisiana, 1997

Aldus Roger, Lafayette, Louisiana, 1982

108

Milton Adams, Kaplan, Louisiana, 2008

Joe "Douglas" Badon, Henderson, Louisiana, 2001

Shelton Manuel, Eunice, Louisiana, 2001

Jason Frey, Eunice, Louisiana, 2008

Visitors of the Crawfish Festival in front of the St. Bernard Cemetery, Breaux Bridge, Louisiana, 1982

Crawfish Festival, Breaux Bridge, Louisiana, 1982

AUTHOR BIO

Emile was born in The Hague, the Netherlands, into a very musical family. As a child he enjoyed playing a toy accordion while wearing his grandfather's hat! Later in life he studied at the Academy of Fine Arts in Breda, the Netherlands, where he earned a Master's Degree with high honors in Photography and Audio Visual Design.

In 1979 he heard unfamiliar music on the Dutch radio—Cajun music from southern Louisiana. It sounded pure and honest.

Three years later Emile traveled to Louisiana to find the Cajun music he had heard on the radio. A portrait series of some pioneer musicians developed and grew with documenting the next generation of younger musicians who were beginning to carry on this Cajun tradition. He traveled a number of times to Louisiana to add more musicians to this photographic collection.

In 2010 the Smithsonian Institution in Washington, D.C., enthusiastically accepted his donation of sixty-four Cajun musician portraits. The Curator of Photography at the Smithsonian, David Haberstich, wrote an article about this donation, "Cajun Music and a Flying Dutchman," which can be found at www.emilecajun.com.

Emile Waagenaar, The Hague, the Netherlands, 1957

INDEX